IT'S *PHISHING* GRANDMA, NOT FISHING

IT'S *PHISHING* GRANDMA, NOT FISHING

****

WEB AND TECH GUIDE

FOR SENIORS

By Maria T.

Table of Contents

Introduction

During the pandemic lockdown, online services and personal and business communications became increasingly necessary, forcing everyone to use technology more permanently. Many processes and interactions did not go turn back to be able to be done in person or the way they used to be, forcing everyone to adjust to the new "normal", becoming necessary for everyone to learn how to deal with this new technology, something not easy for seniors.

Perhaps you don't have much experience using a computer, or a lot of these requirements are new to you, such as the words or computer and technology "language", making it difficult to understand or follow instructions as to how to operate a computer or surf the Web (go online, or on the internet). The purpose of this web and tech dictionary is to explain those most commonly used terms in everyday language to help you understand all the technical language and help you use a computer or smartphone more easily.

The new phone versions are not only made to talk as in the past, but now with a phone, you can send emails, have internet access, and quite a few more features.

Most books that teach how to use computers, or computer programs, have all this technical terminology, which if one does not know what it is or means, makes it harder to learn how to use a computer, phone, or tablet, limiting your ability to take complete advantage of the teaching.

So, this computer/web dictionary comes in handy for a quick at-hand consultation of those terms that are understandable for any novice or senior with little knowledge.

Some of the terms you will find here may not be applicable for your personal and daily use or needed to use a computer, but it is essential to know what they are, mean, and are used for, as it is quite possible you will hear them often. For example, when the technician (or your grandkid) comes to "fix" the internet connection or your computer is being repaired.

This book is organized in alphabetical order for you to find the word or term and its explanation easily and quickly.

I hope you enjoy it and find it handy.

A

ACCOUNT (User)

A generic term used to refer to your access options to services like online baking, utilities, email, or others. Most of these services have you create a user account that leverages a username (e.g., your email or similar) and a password (a set of characters, a passphrase, or another that is only known to you).

AD SIGN

This symbol is used in email addresses to separate the username and the email domain. Think of your email as an address, the characters before the "@" are your username, unique to you as your physical address, and the last part is the service where the email is hosted or stored.

Not every keyboard has the "@" symbol in the same place, even some don't have it, in those cases, you can write it by pressing the "Alt" key and then the number 64. (Shown on most documents as => "Alt+64").

ADOBE®

Adobe® is an American multinational computer software company that produces commonly used programs used by graphic designers to edit photos, videos and design web pages. Also, one of the most common applications to create "pdf" format files.

ANDROID®

This refers to Google's phone operating system (OS), used in google and other brand name phones (e.g., Samsung®). It is the software that the phone uses to work; very much like a computer, today's phones leverage underlying software that not only enables the phone to make calls but also run a multitude of services and applications (apps), like maps, news, music, and other.

You might also hear about its counterpart: iOS, the operating system Apple® branded iPhones use. These 2 are the main OS' and software developers with applications that work for either one of them.

ANTIVIRUS

Part of the programs that make sure your computer is safe and secure, the antivirus program should be running at all times and updated as needed to prevent malicious programs form impacting or getting access to your computer content. It prevents and detects "computer viruses" and "malware software" that could attack the computer.

The software installed on your computer does not come with an antivirus, therefore it is something you need to buy separately. There are quite a few antivirus programs available in the market, which you buy and install online.

APP / APPLICATION (Computer or Mobile Apps)

These are the equivalent of computer programs that you can download onto your smartphone or tablet. There are game apps (e.g., solitaire, driving simulators, star gazing apps), banking applications, social networking apps (e.g., Facebook®, Instagram®, WhatsApp®, etc.), weather apps, and more. Note that some apps are free to download and use, some are free to download but require what's called "in-app payment" for advanced features or services, and some require payment to download and use.

When talking about a computer (laptop, desktop, pc, or mac), the "application" is the computer software installed for a specific use. Some examples include banking software like TurboTax®, image editing software like Photoshop® or internet browsers like Chrome® or Firefox®.

These are also sometimes called computer programs. Most computers come with some applications already installed. The most common examples of pre-installed applications are Microsoft's Word®, Excel®, PowerPoint®, Outlook®, and Google Chrome®.

ARTIFICIAL INTELLIGENCE (AI)

You may have heard about Artificial intelligence, or maybe not. It describes computer algorithms and programs that leverage vast amounts of data to provide answers that seem human-like. These "trained models" are capable of discerning what the human user is asking and replying back with comprehensive and relatively accurate responses so far.

The newest service -ChapGPT- was launched on November 2022 and has become one of the most visited websites ever. It is something that will likely change how we do things today, and probably sooner than we think. The implications of having such tools at hand have raised comments in favor and against it. As it continues its fast development, we will have more knowledge of the pros and cons.

ATTACHMENT

Part of the actions you can take when sending an email is to attach a file (document), a photo or a video when sending it. Those files are called "attachments" as they come along with the email. Attachment can also refer to a file sent via text message via your phone or any social networking app (e.g., WhatsApp®).

B

BACKUP

It is a copy of your files and computer content. It is recommended to keep a backup of your cherished photos or documents in another device such as an external memory or a USB memory card, or you can upload them in the "cloud".

With technology changing daily, the Cloud is an excellent place to save all your information. Some services as Apple® and Google® offer a certain amount of free storage in the Cloud; if more space is needed than what is provided for free, you can always pay for extra storage capacity.

BANDWIDTH

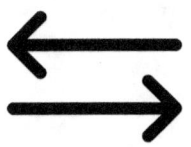

Network bandwidth refers to a measurement that indicates the maximum capacity of your wired or wireless connection. It comprises the total data that can move over a network connection in a certain amount of time. Typically, bandwidth is represented in the number of bits, kilobits, megabits, or gigabits that can be transmitted in 1 second.

BANNER

This refers to the advertising boxes or sections on any given webpage. When you surf the Web, you might see within the page commercial information related to what's included there.

The purpose is to advertise other products, services, or websites for commercial purposes. Clicking on them will take you to a different page than the one you are looking at.

BLOG

Short for "weblog". It is a webpage written and/or a website managed by a person or company to share information, ideas, or opinions. There are different kind of blogs, either run by a person, a business, or a corporation. The information is posted and updated often. Personal bloggers have their own topics like food, travel, health, fitness, and parenting.

Companies and businesses have blogs to advertise their products. Creating and posting a blog is generally free.

BLUETOOTH®

Bluetooth® is a communication technology that enables devices (mobile phones primarily) to communicate between each other and with other gadgets like headsets, speakers, and even your car (if available). This is all done without the need of wires or cables.

Bluetooth connectivity relies on short-range radio frequency; therefore, your devices need to be relatively near to each other to communicate and transfer information.

BOOKMARK (Bookmark Bar)

A (web) bookmark is the equivalent of a bookmark in a book, and these are used to be able to get back to frequently used or visited web pages, e.g., your bank's website, your preferred news outlet, etc. Most browsers commonly only require that you click on the "star" at the end of the address bar to save it.

Once saved, you can find it in the bookmark's menu on top of the browser. You can organize your bookmarks within the browser as if these were files in folders, say a bookmark folder for cooking recipes, a bookmark folder for news outlets, and any other category or grouping you'd like.

BROWSER (Internet)

Program or application that allows you to surf the Web ("internet" and "web" are interchangeable). Most computers come with the browser already installed; most common browsers include Microsoft Edge® (the older version is Internet Explorer®), Google's Chrome®, and Mozilla's Firefox®; these are free to download and use.

When browsing websites, make sure these are "secure"; you can check by looking at the address bar; on the left-hand side there should be a "lock". Also, sometimes the antivirus installed on your computer can block access to a web page if it detects a threat.

C

CACHE

Cache refers to temporary files stored in your computer when you open web pages and applications. Later on, are used by the system to download the content much faster.

CARTRIDGE

The printer cartridge is what contains the ink of the inkjet printers. More modern ones use an ink tank instead of a cartridge. Laser printers use what is known as "toner".

CHAT / CHATTING

Chat or chatting is communicating, interacting, or sending messages over the internet between two or more people. To "chat" you use services like WhatsApp®, iMessage®, Signal®, Telegram®, or Facebook Messenger®. Some of these only work on mobile phones, and some have both phone and computer versions.

In chat services, you can communicate directly with one or more people (groups). It generally happens in real-time. To use a chat app, you need to be connected with Wi-Fi or have a data plan via your cellular communications provider. Most times messages will be free, different than sending SMS messages which might not be. If in doubt check your cell phone data and SMS plan.

CHROME (Google®)

A very popular web browser is used to access the internet, open web pages, and do any search you might need. You would want to install it on your computer, and it is the equivalent of Microsoft's Edge® browser, Firefox® browser, or Safari® browser on Apple® devices. When browsing websites make sure these are "secure", you can check by looking at the address bar, on the left-hand side there should be a "lock".

CISCO WEBEX®

It's the software used to have video chats/conferences in real-time. Similar to Zoom® and Skype®.

CLICK and DOUBLE CLICK

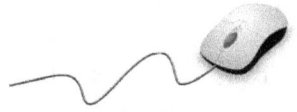

Your mouse has two buttons (some models have 3); typically, you work by clicking around with the left button on icons, links, emails, or apps.

When you are asked to "click on" something, you are being asked to place the mouse arrow on an icon, email address, or a link to open it. Sometimes a single click is needed, others a double click. The action/word "click" becomes important when you hear something like: "don't click an unknown or suspicious message" or "click on the email icon to open the application".

CLOUD (The Cloud)

This term refers to services that store your content (files, photos, media) in a computer/server/data center owned and managed by a company; some of these include iCloud from Apple®, OneDrive from Microsoft®, and Amazon's Prime Photo.

These services allow you to back up your content and transfer it from device to device without needing a USB drive or adding it as an email attachment.

COMPACT DISK

Compact disks (or CDs) are used to store digital content, for a while it was the way to get new computer software installed on your machine; now the prevalent use is files or photos storage in blank CDs. The functionality is the same as USB Drives, with the exception that USB Drives are reusable. Most new computers do not have a CD reader, so using these is no longer common or practical.

COMPUTER FOLDERS and FILES

See "File" and/or "Folders" for more.

COOKIES

This refers to a small piece of code that is stored in your machine every time you visit a website. The purpose of this code is to help your internet browser load the website faster by remembering the information from when you previously visited that site.

Usually, a notice will pop up when you visit a website asking you to "accept or decline cookies" it's best practice to decline most cookies and only accept "essential" cookies. You'll notice that the options include tracking, marketing, and other types of cookies that tend to track your browsing activity across the internet. This can also include "third-party cookies" which is also a good idea to decline.

COPYWRITE / COPYWRITING

With the increased use of the internet for advertising and online sales, crafting written text to better communicate products or services quality has become a new activity and paid job. Think of the text you see when visiting a product on Amazon, donation sites, or other sites. Copywriting is performed by copywriters, who are individuals trained to write the perfect words that will motivate the user to act.

COPYRIGTH©

Copyright refers to the rights given to authors, creators, or other folks that limit what third parties can do with their work product or content. The intent is to protect the copyright owner and make sure others pay when consuming, distributing, copying, displaying, or using it in any way.

An example is music; when an artist creates a musical piece with a copyright, every musician, radio station or music label may only use the music with proper approvals and fees being paid.

CPU

CPU stands for Central Processing Unit, also called Microprocessor. It's the brain of the computer and the most essential part. Its speed and how much RAM (Rapid Access Memory) your machine has will determine how well it performs. CPUs are made by companies like Intel® and AMD®, every model has its specifications which generally are presented in MHz (Megahertz) or GHz (Gigahertz); the higher the number, the faster it is.

D

DATA

GB MB

Data is the measure of "space" used to store messages, photos, apps, and other software on your computer or phone. Also, to measure the amount of content shared over chats, messages, and other communication services.

It is commonly expressed in megabytes and gigabytes (1 Gigabyte = 1,000 Megabytes). Your computer may have a hard drive that can store, for example, 500 gigabytes of data; most phones now can store from 64 up to 256 gigabytes of data (applications, photos, music, and other digital files).

DOMAIN

@hotmail/@gmail

On the internet, the domain usually refers to the address (you could also hear it called a "URL"), either a web page (www.google.com) or an email address (e.g., @hotmail.com, @outlook.com are the domains Microsoft uses for the email service they provide).

DOWNLOAD

To download means to save one or more files on your computer or phone, "copying" them down from the internet. You can download files, documents, photos, and even music from a website, you can also download attachments received in an email. Example: you download your bank statement from your bank's website.

You should be careful when downloading content; make sure you are only downloading content from sites and email senders that you know. The risk is that unknown files/senders could compromise your machine with viruses, ransomware, spam, or spyware. When browsing websites, make sure these are "secure", you can check by looking at the address bar, on the left-hand side there should be a "lock".

E

E-BOOK

Is a digital book, e.g., not printed. These are meant to be read on a computer or any other digital device like a tablet or smartphone. You can find eBooks to download for free from the library website and services like kindle, audible. These two also offer paid downloads and subscriptions to their expanded catalog.

E-COMMERCE (Online Purchasing)

E-Commerce refers to buying and selling goods and/or services over the internet. It can be done via a computer, smartphone, tablet, or any device that can connect to the internet and can access merchant websites or applications, like Amazon, Walmart, or others. Today almost everything is available for purchase online: music, plane tickets, clothing, food, etc. The same happens with services, you can access banking and utilities or even hire someone for odd jobs via some vendor sites.

EMAIL

Email is a message, long or short, personal or business, sent from one person to another using a service such as Hotmail®, Outlook®, or Gmail®.

Emails can include attachments (photos or files).

Emails are delivered extremely fast, once you send them, the email will be received (not necessarily read) almost instantly by the recipient.

EMAIL ACCOUNT

To send and receive emails you need to open an email account with a service of your choice. Gmail, Hotmail, and Outlook are popular ones.

To create an email account, you need to come up with a unique username (myname@exampleemaildomain.com) of your choice and a password, ideally something long (10-12+ characters, known only to you). Once an account is open, you will get your email address with your username, which will look like: myusername@gmail.com. You must remember your password; you will need it every time you access your account.

EMOTICON / EMOJI

With the increase of text-based communications, the rise of emoticons and emojis came about, these are images or characters used to express an emotion; for example, a colon and parenthesis ":)" represents a smiling face.

Both show emotion in a written conversation, by email, message, chat, or other. Emoticons are composed using the letters and punctuation marks on your keyboard (the smiley face above), and emojis are small pictures that can be found via the keyboard of your smartphone or chat service, some emojis can be downloaded from the internet.

EXCEL (Microsoft®)

Created by Microsoft, it's a widely used program in accounting, finance, and general management where spreadsheets are needed to organize numbers and data.

FACEBOOK (By Meta®)

It is a social network, a site where people post and share news or information about their daily life. It is very well-known everywhere and widely used by individuals. To use it, you need to create an account and set up a password. Once you sign in, it can be used on almost any internet-connected device, computer, tablet, iPad, or cell phone. It is used for a wide range of actions, including posting photos, staying in touch with friends, sharing your whereabouts, and comment on other people's posts.

FACETIME®

It is an Apple app and can be used with any apple device connected to the internet (via Wi-Fi or Cell data) which is a significant benefit because you can make "free" internet and video calls to and from any apple device anywhere in the world. As long there is a connection you can use it from home, a hotel, out on the street, or anywhere. If Wi-Fi is unavailable, it will also work using your mobile data plan, in this case, charges may apply.

FILE

A file is a unique document stored on your computer. It could be a document you are working on, say a letter written in Microsoft Word®, or a PDF document or a photo. Files are all identified by the extension after the name; for example, mydocument.doc refers to a Microsoft Word file, and a photo could have the ".jpg" or ".jpeg" extension. (See "File Format" for more information).

FILE FORMAT

Refers to the type of file. If it's a text file, you could hear it's a "word" or "doc" file, which is related to Microsoft's Word® application; or a "pdf" file, which is a text file that can't be edited once it's created. There are hundreds of file formats, and they all correspond to different types of files and how they are used. When browsing the internet, you might see ".html" as the extension type on the webpage.

FIREFOX (Internet Browser)

It is a free web browser for machines that run windows. It offers similar functionality as the one described for Google Chrome and Microsoft Edge.

FOLDER

A folder in a computer is the equivalent of a cabinet with drawers that you might've used to store your paper files and binders. Within the computer, you can create folders to store your files.

G

GAMING (Online Games)

On most devices, you can now download electronic games, card games like solitaire, role-playing games, car racing, and others. Gaming refers to playing games online using a computer, tablet, or mobile phone. It is popular because most can be played by single or multiple players, some are free, and some are paid, and some you can download and play with or without an internet connection. There are pros and cons to playing games online, especially when it has to do with children since there are risks related to addiction and sensitive content being displayed, which could be inappropriate for certain ages.

GIGABYTE

Gigabyte is typically used to measure the amount of stored data or the storage capacity of a device, computer, or phone. The unit symbol for the gigabyte is GB.

For reference:
1,000 Megabyte = 1 Gigabyte = 0,001 Terabytes

GMAIL®

Is the short term for Google Email. It is a free Google service that lets you send and receive emails. Works the same as Hotmail or Outlook (Microsoft's email service), these vary only in the additional services each offer, mostly around online security and total storage available for emails and attachments. As with most internet-based services, to use them, you'll need to create an account with a strong password (10-12 or more characters such as "!@#(*&)".

GOOGLE®

Google is a search engine; you can reach it via your web browser by typing www.google.com in the browser's address bar. It is used to find anything and everything on the internet, the equivalent of what the white and yellow pages used to be. Type any search term and hit enter on your keyboard and a list of results will come up, you can then click on any of those to see the entire web page or navigate to a particular site.

GOOGLE (Chrome®)

A very popular web browser used to access the internet, open web pages, and do any search you might need. It is something that you would want to install on your computer. Other browsers include Microsoft's Edge, the "Firefox" browser from Mozilla Foundation, and "Safari" on Apple devices. When browsing websites, make sure these are "secure", you can check by looking at the address bar, on the left-hand side there should be a "lock".

H

HACK / HACKING / BEING HACKED

Computer systems are vulnerable to hacking, meaning being attacked and interfered with by external people. Hackers access computer systems to gain control, download information, or install malicious software for profit (ransomware). If you are "hacked", it means someone accessed your device or account (e.g., someone "hacked your email" or "hacked your Facebook") with malicious intent. This happens not only to individuals but also to big companies and is also known as a cyberattack.

HARD DRIVE

The hard drive is a component of PCs (Personal Computers) and laptops, it is where digital content (files, photos, videos, etc.) are stored. Also, where the computer applications and programs reside. There are also external hard drives used for storage only.

You might also hear it be called "Computer Memory", it is the same as above, where the information is stored. Without this function, the computer will not work correctly.

HARDWARE

Refers to all the physical components that you can touch or interact with when using your computer, examples include the monitor, the keyboard, the mouse, and the printer. While "system" hardware refers to the internal parts of the computer.

HASHTAG

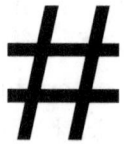

Represented with the # symbol and a word (e.g., #madeinamerica, #newyear), are used to tag posts in blogs, social networking sites (e.g., Facebook, LinkedIn, Instagram), and webpages so that written content that it's related to each other can be searched, filtered and found easily. For example, if you search for #madeinamerica on Facebook, you might find all sorts of merchant pages offering products "Made in America".

If you are using Twitter, the function using the # symbol allows people to follow the topics they are interested in.

In Instagram, the # symbol and combinations of letters, numbers, and/or emoji are used to categorize the content and make it easier to find.

HOTMAIL® and/or OUTLOOK®

Hotmail is a free email service owned and managed by Microsoft, the owner of Outlook as well, that enables you to send and receive email.

Works the same as Gmail (Google's email service), these services vary only in the additional features each offer, primarily around online security and total storage available for emails and attachments. As with most internet-based services, to use them you'll need to create an account with a strong password (10-12 or more characters such as "!@#(*&)".

HOTSPOT

A hotspot is a device used to connect to the internet, it connects to the cellphone network to send and receive data and creates a Wi-Fi network for you to connect your pc, phone, or another device.

There are different models and brands, but most are sold by retailers such as ATT®, VERIZON®, Sprint®, etc. Since these devices use cellular communication to send and receive info, you'll need to sign up for a data plan with your carrier.

You might hear "hotspot" referring to a location where you can connect to the internet as well, this is a common misunderstanding, but the term has become interchangeable in reference to a place (e.g., coffee shop) where an internet connection is available (at cost or not).

Most new phones can also act as hotspots, there are settings in your phone that enable it to create a Wi-Fi network and let other devices connect to it to use your data plan to connect to the internet.

I

iCLOUD (by Apple®)

As mentioned under the description for "Cloud", this is Apple's version of the storage service it offers for its devices. If you have an iPhone, you'll have at least 5 GB of free space where some of your phone content is being backup. Apple offers increased storage capacity along with other services (gaming, music, fitness) via iCloud plans for a fee.

ICON

An icon is a small image that represents a folder or an application on a computer or personal device. If you look at your computer screen, you might see one for the "recycle bin", where files end up if you delete them.

Each represents an action that can be performed by clicking it, either to open a file, a menu, a folder, or a setting.

iOS

It is the operating system developed, owned, and managed by Apple. It is used to run iPhones and devices made by Apple as iPads and Mac Computers. As a user, you only need to know which operating system your device has so that if you download or intend to install an application you get one compatible with it.

IMEI

Every phone has a unique identification or serial number called the IMEI "International Mobile Equipment Identity". This number consists of 15 digits and is useful when your phone gets lost or stolen, it allows the cell phone carrier to block it so no one else can use it. Also, it is helpful when buying a used one to be sure it has not been reported as stolen.

INSTAGRAM (By Meta®, formerly Facebook)

It is a free downloadable app where you can share photos and videos with friends or followers, it's available both for iPhone and Android phones. It allows the user to create a profile and share it across other social platforms like Facebook and Twitter as well.

INTERNET (The Web)

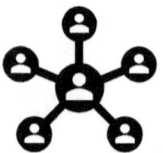

It's the "global system of interconnected computer networks that uses the Internet protocol suite (TCP/IP)[b] to communicate between networks and devices." ([1])

This standard protocol allows computers (servers) owned by a multitude of entities (private, public, non-profit) to share and host information for everyone to access, some for free and some for-profit (behind paywalls with subscriptions or 1-time fees).

IP ADDRESS

The IP (internet protocol) address is a unique set of numbers assigned and used to identify each of your internet-connected devices (computer, phone, printer); this assignment happens automatically when you connect to the internet.

---

[1] Source https://en.wikipedia.org/wiki/Internet

iPAD®

It is Apple's "tablet" and brand name. All Apple devices operate with Apple's iOS system. The iPad has a lot of functions: receive emails, log to the internet, take notes and many others.

iTUNES®

Part of the Apple software portfolio is being discontinued. Those services have moved to Apple Music, Apple Podcasts, Apple TV, and Apple Books, where you can listen, view or download music, videos, podcasts, and audiobooks. People who had paid subscriptions to iTunes can now access the content in these other apps.

J

JPG

Refers to a file format (file type) generally used for photos or images. It is one of the most popular formats for storing photos because it compresses the images, so the file tends to be small, making it easy to share over email, messages, or other applications.

Other file types similar to jpg, and associated with images include: "ai", "bmp", "dng", "gif", "heic", "jpeg", "jpg", "png", "raf", "raw", "tif" and "tiff" to name a few.

K

KEYBOARD

It's a hardware component used to type in a computer, not very dissimilar to typewriters but with added functionality (in the image above, you can see there are function buttons, a number keypad on the right side and arrow keys, to name a few).

Not all keyboards display the keys in the same place as the old typewriters did, but in the end, they all have the same basic functions. Also, old typewriter keyboards, regardless of the brand, were all displayed the same, that does not happen with computer keyboards, they can differ from brand to brand.

L

LINK

Some refer to it as a Link or hyperlink. It is a piece of text, numbers, or similar that corresponds to a location (page, document, webpage, URL) on the internet.

For example:

www.google.com is the URL (uniform resource locator) for Google's search engine main page, clicking in such link would help you navigate to that page.

On a website, a link or hyperlink takes you to other webpages or resources, even different locations on the internet (for example: within google.com you search for the name of your favorite actor/actress, and the search results bring up links to news articles, which in turn provide links to a movie trailer or videos, all hosted in different locations).

You might receive links via email or phone message. Before clicking on these links, make sure you know who the sender is and what they are asking you to click, as this is a common way fraudsters use to attempt phishing. If you are not sure about the origin of the link is best to delete the message/email, as clicking on it could allow the attacker to compromise your machine, access your information, or install malicious code (malware, spyware) on your device.

LINUX®

It's an operating system like Windows. It differs from it in that it's "open source", meaning it's free to use and maintained by volunteers that work to upkeep the program.

This is usually unavailable as the default operating system on end-user computers, which come with either Windows (PCs) or iOS on Apple devices.

LOG-IN / Logging

It refers to using the username assigned to you for any given service along with the password to access the service.

For example:

- your banking website will require a username and a password, when you go to the website or open the application and type both, you are logging in to it.

- if you have an email account, when you go to the provider (Hotmail, Gmail), you are asked to log in.

MALWARE

Refers to malicious software or programs designed to do damage to a computer. Malware includes various malicious programs like spyware, trojan horses, viruses, etc.

MEDIA PLAYER

Media players: it's an application that enables you to listen to music or other media, allowing you to play MP3 files (the standard music file format) or watch movies (which generally use the .mov file extension). Windows Media Player and iTunes are popular media players.

MEGABYTE

The word comes from a measurement in the metric system equivalent to one million. A megabyte is typically used to measure the amount of stored data or the storage capacity of a device, computer, or phone. The unit symbol for the megabyte is MB.

For reference:
1,000 Megabytes = 1 Gigabyte = 0,001 Terabytes

MEMORY CARD

See SD CARD

MESSAGES – Also known as SMS

It is a text sent from one phone to another and can come from a friend, family member, or unknown source. They are also used by banks and businesses to send alerts or promotions.

MESSENGER

It is an app used to send private text messages over the internet between two or more people that you will need to download to your phone or computer.

MICROSOFT EDGE®

It is a free web browser for windows. It offers similar functionality as described for Google Chrome and Mozilla Firefox.

MICROPROCESSOR

It is another name for the CPU; it is the "brain of a computer".

MMS MESSAGE

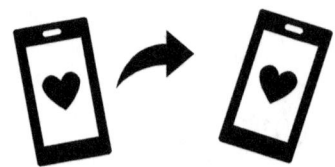

Stands for Multimedia Messaging Service. A message that includes something like a file, a photo, an emoji or a web page link is known as an MMS.

MODEM

To access the internet, you need a modem that connects your home network to your internet service provider (ISP). In conjunction with a router, it lets all your electronic devices, either wired or wireless, use that same internet connection at once and also if needed or wanted each device can talk to one another directly.

MONITOR

It is the computer screen, usually an external hardware component. It will be attached if your device is a laptop or other portable device.

MOUSE

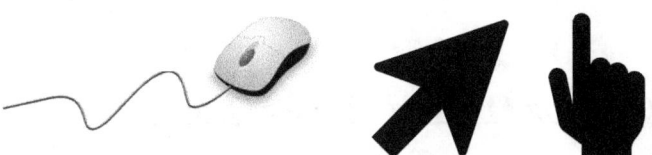

It's the hardware component that allows you to move a cursor around the screen. It is used alongside the keyboard to operate programs and applications. When moving the mouse across the screen it changes its form (vertical line when you are writing, an arrow when pointing at something, etc.).

The mouse can have a cord (wired) that connects to your device or be a newer model without a cable (wireless). Laptops also have what is called a "trackpad", a section of the board where you touch with your finger to move the pointer or cursor around the screen.

N

NETWORKING

It is when computers are connected to each other so they can share information. For example, in a bank or company.

O

ONLINE (Getting Online or Being Online)

When you are logged in, surfing, or connected to the internet.

ONLINE APPLICATION

There is an extensive range of online applications, but in short words is a program you would use on a computer that is actively connected to the internet. Examples of these include multiplayer games, where you are actively playing with other people simultaneously via the internet.

OPERATING SYSTEM (OS)

Main software of the computer which comes pre-installed. Most popular ones are Windows (for PCs), Linux, and Apple OS X (for Mac or other Apple devices).

OUTLOOK®

Outlook is Microsoft's email service, initially known as Hotmail. It is free for personal use and gives you 15GB of storage. Outlook is a competitor of Gmail.

P

PASSWORD

It is a combination of characters, numbers, and symbols that is unique and only known to you. Along with your username, you leverage the password to gain access to internet services and applications.

For example, your online banking portal requires a username and a password. For security reasons is recommended that for each service, you use a unique password and that you do not share it with anyone.

To increase security, you can leverage passphrases, a combination of random words that extend the length of your password, for example, "card pink Canada". The longer the password, the better.

PC (Personal Computer)

A personal computer is one designed to be used by one person. There are two kinds: desktop computers and laptop computers. A Desktop typically consists of a "tower", where the hard drive and other internal components live and external hardware (monitor, keyboard, mouse, etc.). Some newer desktop models come without a tower, they only have the monitor and the keyboard.

A laptop is a portable device, a single machine that doesn't require anything to operate (other than access to a power connection to charge the battery). Most laptops today are designed to perform the same functions as a desktop.

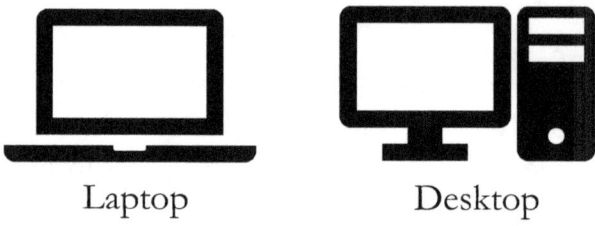

Laptop   Desktop

PDF (File or Document)

PDF is a file format (Equivalent to Microsoft's .doc for word files or ppt for PowerPoint files). This unique extension is used for files that, once created, can't be modified. As with any other files, these can be sent as attachments via email and stored in cloud services.

PHISHING

Phishing is the name given to a new recurring and frequent fraudulent practice that entails sending emails or other messages that appear to be from reputable companies to trick individuals into revealing personal information such as passwords and credit card numbers.

This practice generally requires sending emails, text messages, or other online communications that look as real as possible but include links to fake websites or applications, where the target is tricked into typing usernames and passwords for their accounts.

Typical cases include fraudulent emails requesting you log into bank accounts, social media, or even work applications. Sometimes these emails can appear as "wonderful offers" or stating there is a problem with your bank or email accounts, and they will be "blocked" if the message is not replied right away.

The safest thing to do is not to open them and delete them if you do not recognize the sender or you have not requested assistance.

PINTEREST®

It is also considered a social media platform like Facebook or Instagram; the difference is Pinterest is focused on providing inspiration using images (photos). On their platform, you can find ideas for home decoration, cooking, sewing, and a lot more. Subscription is free, you will need to create a password.

PLAYSTORE (Google)

It is Google's App Store, where users with Android devices can download things such as applications, games, and music. It is for Android cell phones only; there is an Apple Store for Apple devices (iPhones). Some of the applications and games found in these stores are free to use, some require purchasing, and some even are partially free, requiring in-app purchases for extended functionality.

PLUGINS also PLUG-IN

They are add-on software extensions that can be downloaded to the computer, such as Adobe Acrobat, Adobe Flash, and Java.

These complement functionality in the internet browser allowing for enhanced services, information, and other specialty functions on some websites.

PODCAST

Just as there are magazine subscriptions, free or paid, there are now subscriptions you can sign up to listen to audio files created by different people and organizations. These audio recordings can be for any sort of topic, including education, politics, culture, science and entertainment included.

Most of these audio files can be played from the websites where they are displayed or stored or via specialty applications (e.g., Google's podcasts, Apple's iTunes). Some "creators" now offer both audio and video, called Webcast.

POP-UP ADDS

These are the small windows with advertising that sometimes come up (pop-ups) when you are visiting a website or when you open a web page. Usually, the purpose is to sell something to you.

Some well-known companies use pop-ups, but there are also "bad ads" which can infect your computer and steal your personal information. If you are not sure if it is a reliable source, it is better not to click them and close the pop-up browser window.

PORT (Computer Ports)

The port or docking point in a computer or laptop is where you can connect other devices to the computer: the mouse, a printer, a scanner or any other device. These are standardized for each purpose. Some standard ports are Universal Serial Bus ports, USB-C ports, Ethernet ports or Display Port.

PORTAL

Web pages have evolved, and as the functionality increases, you might hear references to a "web portal". A portal is a generic term for websites that generally require a username and password to access and offer unique services.

An example of this is your "banking portal", the main page is visible to anyone, but you can only access information about your accounts via the portal if you can authenticate yourself via username and password.

Government entities also use portals to provide information about taxes, jobs available, and other information of interest to the public.

POWER BUTTON

The power button is the on/off switch on the computer; phones and tablets generally have a small round button on one side to turn on/off the device. Not all have it in the same place, and depending on the model, some computers might have it in the back; laptop computers can have it by the keyboard.

POWERPOINT (By Microsoft®)

It is one of Microsoft's available programs to create presentations with graphics, audio, and photos.

PROFILE

Refers to your personal information on any given service on the internet. Companies require you to complete some basic (or extended) profile to leverage within their applications. A great example of this is Facebook, where you are asked to provide information such as your birth date, location, and other personal information to better serve your interest and "connect" you with like-minded people. In most cases, it's better to provide the least information possible.

PROFILING

The personal information gathered by companies while you are using the internet can be bought and sold (depending on the terms of use of each application/vendor) and then aggregated and used for many things, including sending you advertisements while you are online.

QR CODE

Similar to barcodes at supermarkets (used to identify a product and its price when read in a cash register), QR codes are intended to be read (via your phone's camera) and direct you to a location on the internet.

Even though the technology was created years ago, it is now starting to be widely used. You will see it everywhere; in any kind of certificate, product, listing, poster, cards, boxes, airline boarding pass, etc. The code can contain different kinds of information, a restaurant menu, a web page, a video, a message, and many more alternatives. It works with your smartphone camera.

To "read" a QR Code, you place your smartphone camera pointing to the code, and without taking a picture, place your finger anywhere on the phone screen, and right away, a new window will open up on your phone, showing the information that the code points to. To create a code, you use free services such as https://www.qr-code-generator.com

R

RAM

It stands for "random access memory". RAM is a computer memory that can be read and changed in any order, typically used to store working data and machine code. This is a word you will infrequently hear, only if you are shopping for a new computer or updating the old one, as it is an integral part of the machine's specifications.

ROUTER

To access the internet, you need a modem that connects your home network to your internet service provider (ISP). In conjunction with a router, it lets all electronic devices, wired or wireless, use that internet connection simultaneously and allows them to talk to one another directly.

S

SAFARI (By Apple®)

It is Apple's web browser and was developed specifically for all apple devices: iPhones, iPads and Mac Computers. It comes pre-installed in all Apple products.

SCAN / SCANNING

Most paper documents can now be digitized via the use of a scanner machine or even via mobile phone applications that take a photo and create a digital version of it.

A Scanned file is usually saved as a pdf (not in all cases) and can then be stored, emailed, or attached to any other service (email, cloud storage, etc.). Scans can be done in color or black and white, different sizes, etc., but all depends on the features of the scanner.

SCREENSHOT

A screenshot is a capture of an image or content displayed on the screen. You can screenshot web pages and save the file in similar formats to photos.

Each machine has a different way of taking screenshots, in Windows-based devices, you can search for the "snip and sketch" tool to screenshot content.

SD CARDS (Memory cards, USB Sticks)

SD Cards (secure digital cards), also known as "memory cards", are used to store files in a small portable format.

You can find SD cards from multiple vendors that use similar technology but offer various sizes and storage capacity. SD cards are primarily used in small electronic devices like cameras. It is where the photos will be stored when using such devices. You can then read the SD card in your computer (if it has the appropriate port) and copy them to the computer, have them printed, or delete them from the SD card. For phones and other devices, usually, the SD card is smaller and called Micro SD.

SEARCH ENGINE

These are web-based tools that allow you to find almost everything on the internet.

Today the top search engines include:

Google: www.google.com
Microsoft's Bing: www.bing.com
Yahoo: www.yahoo.com
Ask: www.ask.com
DuckDuckGo: www.duckduckgo.com

Once you type the name into the address bar, you will see a search bar, a space where to type the text or item you want to search for, once you hit enter, you will see a list of results where you can pick what to read next.

SHOPPING CART

When shopping online, the shopping cart will always be there, the icon is similar on all web pages and is where you'd click once you have picked your products and you are ready to pay and check out from that particular store.

SIGNAL®

It is a similar application to WhatsApp, a chatting and audio/video calling service. With Signal, you can share photos, written messages, and videos. To connect with other people, the recipient must also have the Signal App installed. Other names in this category include Skype, Telegram, and Microsoft Messenger.

SIM CARD

The SIM card is only for mobile phones, it is very tiny and looks like a chip, all phones have one, and is installed by your phone carrier. It contains all the information about the phone and your account.

SIRI (By Apple®)

Siri is a virtual assistant available on Apple devices, iPhone, Apple Watch, and iPad. With Siri, you can interact with the phone or device by using your voice to search or start applications.

When you talk to Siri, it will talk back to you and confirm the instruction you've provided. If enabled, Siri has access to all your applications on your device; therefore, you can give her commands or ask questions all hands-free.

Siri is very useful for people with disabilities. It is voice-activated and can read back to the user the content displayed on their iPhone.

SKYPE®

It is software used to communicate in real time, either by video, chat, or messages, people still use it, but now it is less popular and is being replaced by Microsoft Teams and other platforms.

SMS (Text messages)

It stands for "Short Message Service". Usually, a single text message is limited to 160 characters, including spaces. Most devices now have capabilities that expand and allow for MMS, which stands for Multimedia Messaging Service.

These MMS allow users to send images, videos, or audio via a traditional cellular network. This was a common way of sending pictures, also known as Picture Messages, to friends and colleagues before mobile applications began using mobile Internet networks to send larger files.

SOCIAL MEDIA – SOCIAL NETWORKS

Social Media refers to applications and platforms that allow for sharing and communicating, keeping in touch with friends and family, and browsing content posted by others, actions are called Social Networking.

Facebook, Twitter, Snapchat, and Instagram are the most common social networks, but there are many more. Some promote interacting with different or more specific purposes, like LinkedIn, which connects people for work and business, or dating websites to find a match.

SOCIAL MEDIA PLATTFORM

It is any site on the internet that allows people to connect and share ideas or interests. There is a wide variety of them: blogs, instant messaging, and podcasts among others.

SOFTWARE

It's the code and programs that are executed (run) via the hardware. When you turn on your computer, the software is the set of instructions that helps the different components of the PC work and communicate with each other and allow it to carry out tasks.

SMILEYS

An emoji that depicts a round face (happy-sad-surprised) is used in written messages with other Emoticons or emojis to show a specific emotion.

SNAPCHAT®

Even though it is similar to the other Apps for texting and talking to friends, Snapchat has quite a few different features, for example, you can send a photo to a friend and set it to disappear after a couple of seconds from when it was viewed by the recipient. It works both with Android and Apple phones.

SPAM

This term refers to unwanted and unsolicited emails received by users with advertising or commercial promotions for goods and services. You can also find it in your email service as a folder called "junk" mail, a simile to the physical junk mail you might get in your mailbox.

SPOTIFY®

It's an application to listen to music, podcasts, and other files with some limitations, mainly advertising. When you do not pay for a subscription, you cannot download music and will have occasional interruptions with pop-up advertising. This application requires a Wi-Fi connection to access the content.

The company offers a paid subscription called "Prime Spotify" where you will have no advertising and can download music to listen to at any time without a Wi-Fi connection.

SPYWARE

It is another malicious software that can be installed on your computer without your permission. It hides on the computer operating system and makes unwanted changes in the computer.

STREAMING – LIVE STREAM

Is the transmission using the internet of a live event that any person can see via a computer or mobile devices, such as a concert, news, or anything played in real-time (live streaming) or that has been previously recorded (streaming). There are stream platforms you can subscribe to listen to music or watch movies, like Spotify, Netflix, or Apple Music.

T

TABS

The word "Tab" can refer to:

The various browser windows: located at the top of the screen in the browser, allow you to click on them with the mouse to open another page.

The "tab" key on the keyboard.

TABLET

As technology has evolved, new devices have come to the market, one of these is Tablets; they look like larger mobile phones (square and flat) but are somewhat larger in size.

Just like laptops and computers, these tablets can perform multiple functions (web browsing, document storage) and connect to the internet or other devices (printers). While models and features vary between manufacturers, most of the basic functionality is common to all. Every time new models come out, usually come with more features.

TEAMS (Microsoft®)

"Teams" was developed by Microsoft. It is an app designed for communication in real-time. This app can be accessed for free (with limited functionality) or via a paid subscription. The platform has useful features for business communications as it allows online meetings and document sharing.

TELEGRAM®

It is another chat, voice, and video communication application; it is similar to WhatsApp and Signal. It allows you to send text, images, and voice messages or make voice and video calls. They are mostly used in Asia, Europe, and Latin America.

To connect with other people, the recipient must also have the Telegram App installed. Other names in this category include Skype and Microsoft Messenger.

TEXT MESSAGES - SMS

It stands for "Short Message Service". Usually, a single text message is limited to 160 characters, including spaces. Most devices now have capabilities that expand and allow for MMS, which stands for Multimedia Messaging Service. These MMS allow users to send images, videos, or audio via a traditional cellular network. This was a common way of sending pictures, also known as Picture Messages, to friends and colleagues before mobile applications began using mobile Internet networks to send larger files.

TIK TOK®

It is a social media app or platform, very popular among young people, where they post music and short dancing videos of them. It is free to download. Users must be at least 13 years old.

TOOLBAR

The toolbar is a section within most applications that hold icons to execute different functions; in MS Word, for example, you'll find it at the top, including menus for "inserting" content into your document, for "formatting" it, and also a "help" menu.

TOUCH SCREEN

Your mobile phone's screen is a "touch screen". With your finger, you can touch and select, start, and run applications within the device. Some computers now also have touchscreens, so users can easily manipulate and interact with the content and applications.

TWITTER®

Twitter is a social media application. Once you open an account, you can post short messages (up to 280 characters). They are used widely by celebrities, politicians, and almost anyone to share their thoughts and ideas. These short messages are also called tweets.

As with most social media applications, you select who to "follow" and can also be "followed" by others. Meaning that once you open the application you will see a feed or stream of posts by those you select to follow.

TWO-FACTOR AUTHENTICATION (2FA) and MULTIFACTOR AUTHENTICATION (MFA)

2FA and MFA refer to secondary security checks that are intended to protect your accounts from unauthorized access. Usually, you'd use only your username and password to enter or log in to a service, since these can be potentially compromised, some websites and applications offer an additional (2FA or MFA) step to verify you are indeed the correct owner of the account, these additional security steps could be one of more of the following:

- Having the application/service send you a text message to your phone with a code (SMS).

- Using an "authenticator" app that generates a unique code.

- Use a "hardware-based key" that contains or generates a one-time-use-only code for authentication.

U

UPLOAD

This means moving or copying a document, photo, or another file from one device (e.g., your phone or computer) into a website or application. For example, you upload your work resume online using the company's form; similarly, when you access Facebook and post a photo, you are "uploading" it into that service.

USB PORT

Most computers come with USB ports (universal serial bus ports), which are generally located on the side or back of the machine. A port is a hardware component used to connect another device, in this case, one with a matching USB plug, like a mouse or external screen.

There are various types of USB ports, USB-A and USB-C are the most used.

USB CARD – USB DRIVES

USB-A

See SD Cards

URL

URL stands for Uniform Resource Locator. A URL is the address of a given unique resource on the Web (e.g., www.google.com, www.discovery.com)

USERNAME

The username is the one you have chosen to log in to a service or application (email or web page). Most of the time to log in, both the username and the password are required. Most sites ask to create a unique username (name, email, or other).

V

VIRUS (Computer Virus)

Refers to malicious software that spreads through networks and computers. There are many kinds of viruses, some can be very harmful and impact a computer's normal operation. Your computer can get infected by a virus in different ways, most coming is by opening an email attachment from unknown senders or visiting infected web pages.

Within the wide variety of viruses' as of late, the most heard of are malware, "trojans" and "worms". Having an anti-virus installed, constantly updated, and running all the time on the computer is key to preventing issues with your machine. A reliable good quality anti-virus is recommended.

VOICE MAIL

Even though there are voicemails and voice messages, and technically speaking are different, in the end, they work the same way, it is a verbal message sent to you, most of the time to your phone, that you can listen to at a later date and time.

VPN

VPN stands for Virtual Private Network. The VPN is a service that establishes a secure connection to the internet via a 3rd party vendor, so your activity on the internet cannot be tracked by the sites you visit. It Could be useful when using public networks. It does not come with computer programs; it is something you will need to subscribe to and pay a monthly fee.

WEB (Worldwide Web, www)

The "Web" and the "internet" are different things, the internet is the network to which computers are connected, and the Web (www) is the pages you can access or open via the internet.

WEB BROWSER

See (internet) Browser.

WEB PAGE

Speaking in tech terms, the web page is a written document you can see and read online, while the website is a collection of pages located in the same domain.

WEBINAR – WEB SEMINAR

It is an online live event or conference that many people can attend at once. Sometimes are also called online seminars. These can be recorded or not.

You can access webinars via different platforms, directly from webpages, or via communication services like Zoom, Skype, Teams, and others.

Sometime before the seminar/conference takes place, the host will send you the invitation to be able to log in, it consists of the link and the conference or seminar ID. Some of these platforms are also being used for private and personal events among family and friends.

WEBSITE

A collection of web pages located in the same domain. Usually, all with a similar related topic(s) and are linked under the same domain address. (e.g., News by www.nytimes.com)

Wi-Fi

Wi-Fi is a common term to describe available connectivity to the internet. Refers to a common set of standards used to connect devices between them. This sign is displayed somewhere on your device when connected to the internet.

WhatsApp®

Free communication application that allows for text messages (chat), video, and voice communications over the internet. Widely used to connect with friends and family. You can join individually with one person or make groups. When using the group feature, the creator is the administrator and the person who invites others to join, accept, remove, or deny access to an individual. With this app, you can text, send photos and videos, verbal messages or make phone and video calls.

If you are invited to join a group, you can accept or decline the invitation, also if in a group you can leave it any time you wish.

WIDGETS

Similar to an App, the difference is the user does not need to download it to use it or make it run. Common widgets are weather, calendar, clock, and battery. Widgets can be found on the computer but are more common on phones and provide simpler, quicker data.

WINDOWS

It's a computer operating system created by Microsoft, similar to Apple's OS and Linux. It is the most common default operating system on end-user computers (PCs).

X

X-BOX®

It is a hardware console created and owned by Microsoft to play games online and offline. To be able to use it you need to create a Microsoft account, have a good internet connection (for online games), a TV or monitor with HDMI, and the Xbox console. To know if your TV has HDMI, you can check the ports in the back of the TV and see if one is labeled "HDMI".

Y

YAHOO® (Email, Search engine)

Originally one of the initial search engines available when the internet was created. The company then pivoted business models to offer email, search, and other related functionality (www.yahoo.com).

YOUTUBE®

It is a platform that allows people to upload videos and share them with others. It is very popular and free for anyone to watch those videos. People create their "channels" where they will have "followers".

Z

ZIP FILE

A zip file refers to a "compressed" file, one that uses a particular technology to reduce the size (in megabytes) so that it can be shared more easily.

Some services (email, social media) have limitations as to the maximum size a file can be to be transferred via their application (e.g., a big video, multiple pages), so an alternative you can explore is to compress the file(s) into a Zip file format to reduce the size. You can find programs to compress (zip) files on the open internet.

<u>ZOOM®</u>

It's a communications platform primarily intended for corporate use that allows for text, video, and voice communication. Similar to Microsoft Teams and Google Meets.

It enables people to have real-time online meetings either with friends or for work. Zoom, like other platforms, has a free version and a paid one. You can join a Zoom meeting both on your computer and on your mobile device by downloading the app.

Summary

Below is a grouping of the most common services used by category:

Social Media:

Facebook®
YouTube®
Instagram®
LinkedIn®
Snapchat®
TikTok®
Twitter®

Communications (Video, audio, chat):

Zoom®
Microsoft Teams®
Slack®
Webex (by Cisco) ®
FaceTime (by Apple®)
Messenger (by Meta®)
Signal®

Skype®
Telegram®
WhatsApp®
WeChat®